D0367919

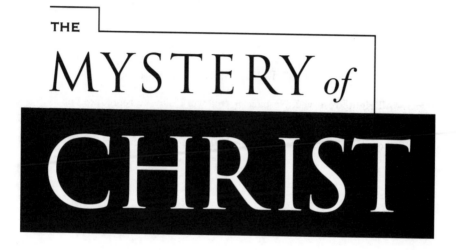

THE
MYSTERY *of*
CHRIST

WATCHMAN NEE

Living Stream Ministry
Anaheim, California

© 1997 Living Stream Ministry

All rights reserved. No part of this work may be reproduced or transmitted in any form or by any means—graphic, electronic, or mechanical, including photocopying, recording, or information storage and retrieval systems—without written permission from the publisher.

First Edition, June 1997.

ISBN 1-57593-954-1

Published by

Living Stream Ministry
1853 W. Ball Road, Anaheim, CA 92804 U.S.A.
P. O. Box 2121, Anaheim, CA 92814 U.S.A.

Printed in the United States of America

97 98 99 00 01 02 / 9 8 7 6 5 4 3 2 1

CONTENTS

PREFACE

This book contains a series of messages given by Watchman Nee in Shanghai in 1939 on the mystery of Christ. The contents are from notes by K. H. Weigh.

Chapter One

THE MYSTERY OF CHRIST

Scripture Reading: Eph. 3:4-6; John 12:32; Luke 12:50-52

THE MYSTERY HIDDEN IN THE AGES

In Ephesians 3:4-6 Paul speaks of his understanding of the mystery of Christ. This mystery was not made known to the sons of men in other generations. The men of old did not know of the mystery that God spoke through Paul, which involves the Jews and Gentiles becoming one new man in Christ Jesus. This is the corporate Christ, which is the church. Verse 6 of chapter three is a precious verse. The words "fellow members" refer to the new man in Ephesians 2:15. The new man stands in contrast to the old man. There are many individual men in this world, but there is only one old man. In the same way, there are many Christians, but there is only one new man—the church.

ONE NEW MAN

In order to understand what the new man is, we must first understand what the old man is. The old man is the God-created man who fell through sin. Every person in Adam is not only a sinner before God, but also an old man. When such a sinner, the old man, hears the gospel and believes in Christ and is saved, he becomes a new man. Not only has he become a new man individually; he is joined to all other Christians to become one corporate new man as well. Ephesians 1 speaks of the church as the Body of Christ; chapter two speaks of the church as the new man; chapter three speaks of the mystery of Christ; chapter four speaks of the way to build up the Body of Christ; chapter five speaks of the responsibility of the church; and chapter six speaks of the warfare of the church. The peak of God's work is the church, which is the new man. God saves us so that we will become a new man in Christ.

A great lack among Christians today is that everyone wants to be an individual Christian. Everyone wants to be good and zealous; everyone wants to sit and listen to good sermons. In short, everyone wants to be a Christian in an individual way. But God does not just want us to be good on an individual basis. He is after a corporate vessel that will destroy Satan and accomplish His plan. God does not want to see Christians scattered like a pan of sand. He wants Christians to be joined together to become a corporate new man.

WHAT IS THE NEW MAN?

Ephesians 2 speaks of Christ creating one new man out of two groups of people, but it does not tell us what the new man is like. According to Colossians 3:10-12, the new man is renewed unto full knowledge according to the image of Him who created him. In the new man there is no Greek or Jew, circumcision or uncircumcision, barbarian or Scythian, slave or free man, but Christ is all and in all. The new man is not a matter of having or not having distinctions; it is a matter of either being the new man or being nothing. The new man is not in the realm of being a Greek or a Jew. The new man is simply Christ. The nature of the new man is Christ. In the new man Christ is all and in all. We can even venture to say that Christ is the church and the church is Christ, because everything in the new man—the church—is simply Christ. The constitution of the new man is nothing less than Christ Himself.

THE CHURCH BEING CHRIST

Since the nature of the new man—the church—is Christ, we can say that the church is Christ. Let us read two passages. In Luke 12:50-52 the Lord said, "I have a baptism to be baptized with,…Do you think that I have come to give peace on the earth? No, I tell you, but rather division." Why did the Lord say this? He said this because He had said that

He would cast fire on the earth. This fire is the fire of God's life. This means He would release His life on the earth to all those who would believe in Him so that they would be regenerated and receive God's life. This matter, however, could only be accomplished after His baptism, which refers to His crucifixion. John 12 reveals that the church is produced out of Christ's death and resurrection. He is the grain of wheat that fell into the earth, died, and brought forth many grains—the church—in resurrection. From these two passages we can see that the church is produced by the life of Christ. Through His death and resurrection, Christ released His life and dispensed it into the believers. These believers are then joined together to become the church.

THE CHURCH BEING THE CORPORATE CHRIST

In the New Testament there are two ways to look at Christ. On the one hand, He is Jesus Christ the Nazarene—this is the individual Christ. On the other hand, He is Christ plus the church—the corporate Christ. First Corinthians 12:12 refers to the second aspect when it says, "All the members of the body, being many, are one body, so also is the Christ." Anything apart from Christ is not the church. There is only one thing in a Christian that forms a part of the church—Christ. The church is the corporate Christ. In the church there is only Christ. During the bread-breaking meeting, the portion that we break off from the whole still signifies the Body of Christ, the church. The church is not what is added to Christ but what issues out from Christ.

Today there are divisions among God's children because there are differences in organizations, personal views, concepts, choices, preferences, and doctrines. But in God's eyes the church is inseparable. All these differences are merely outward differences; they are not differences in the intrinsic reality of the church. The church is the composition of all the believers with Christ. The church is the corporate Christ. When all the saints are joined together in Christ, we have the church. Since there is only one Christ, there can be only one church. Hence, it is indivisible and inseparable.

CHAPTER TWO

THE BODY OF CHRIST

Scripture Reading: Eph. 3:4-6; Col. 3:4-11; Rom. 12:3-5

THE CHURCH BEING THE BODY OF CHRIST

In this message we will speak on the Body of Christ. In the New Testament, Paul was the only apostle who used the expression *the Body of Christ* to denote the church. In other places in the New Testament, the church is called the temple of God, the household of God, etc. But Paul specifically said that the church is the Body of Christ. The subject here is not us becoming the sons of God or becoming Christians. We are talking about how the church becomes the Body of Christ. We can say that the church is Christ in a different form. Christ was the only begotten Son of God. Now He has become the Firstborn. Christ plus all the sons—the church—is the one Body. There are no individual persons in the church; there is only Christ in the church. Anything that issues from Christ is the church. The church comes fully out of Christ and is one with Christ. There is no need for a Christian to do anything or change anything in order to be in Christ. As long as a man is regenerated, he is in Christ and becomes a part of the Body of Christ.

THE BODY OF CHRIST BEING A MATTER OF LIFE

The church as the Body of Christ is absolutely a matter of life. The church as the Body of Christ is not a doctrine; it is of life. A man cannot become a part of the Body of Christ just by understanding it. He becomes a part of the Body of Christ through regeneration. This is absolutely a matter of life; it has nothing to do with knowledge or doctrine. As Christians we need very much to see the Body of Christ.

But the only way we can see the Body of Christ is by God's revelation. We cannot understand the Body of Christ with our mind. Even if we have all the knowledge there is about the Body of Christ, we still may not have seen the Body of Christ or touched the reality of the Body. Only those who have received revelation from God will see the Body of Christ, and only they will enter the reality of the Body.

Romans 12 tells us that the church is the Body of Christ, but it does not explain how the church becomes the Body of Christ. In order to understand how the church becomes the Body of Christ, we have to understand Romans 5 through 8. Chapter five tells us that all men are joined to Adam and that man derives his life from Adam. Through Adam's fall, all men have become sinners and have been joined to the old man. Chapter six tells us that the old man has to be dealt with; it has to be crucified with Christ. Through Christ's redemption, we have died and resurrected. Chapter seven says that a man should no longer live according to the flesh but according to the Spirit. Chapter eight goes on to explain how we live according to the Spirit.

THE BODY OF CHRIST BEING
THE CONSUMMATION OF THE WORK OF THE CROSS

The consummation of the work of the cross is the church. The work of the cross goes as far as the Body of Christ and consummates with the Body of Christ. Hence, the knowledge of the cross brings us to the knowledge of the Body of Christ. The cross brings a man to a state of weakness and inability, one in which he totally loses hope in the old creation. When he is brought to this point, he is delivered in a real way from the old creation and brought into the new creation. Everything in the old creation has been condemned and terminated by the cross. The Body of Christ is the new creation; it has nothing to do with the old creation. If we resort to human methods, tactics, and skills (which we have used in the past) to deal with the affairs of the church, the result will only be disastrous. God does not approve of anything that is from the old creation, and He will not allow anything from the old creation to remain in the new creation. Everything of the old creation must pass through the cross and remain on the cross. The church has no use for anything that comes from the old man. The church only takes that which issues from Christ.

When man fell, he fell because of his own concepts, choices, and judgments. Therefore, God will not allow anything that issues from the old creation to gain the upper hand. The "backbone" of the natural man must be broken; the hollow of his thigh must be touched. Before he will submit to God, he must be crippled and fall flat on his face. This is what God is doing in the new creation. He is smashing everything of the old creation, and He is constituting us with everything that issues from Christ so that we can become the Body of Christ in practicality. I saw the evil of man's flesh twelve years ago in Philippians 3, Romans 5, and John 5. For seven months I was hesitant to make any move at all, because I knew that everything that issued from the flesh would be rejected by God. God wants to remove everything in man that is from the flesh. God's children must first deal with the natural life. If they deal with their natural life, they will be in the Body spontaneously, because the Body of Christ is composed of everything that issues from Christ. Nothing of the old man can remain in the Body. As soon as a man passes through the experience in Romans 5 through 8, he can enter into the experience of Romans 12.

Today the church is divided because Christians are living in the wrong realm and the wrong sphere. Christians are not living in the new creation or in the reality of the Body of Christ. They are living only in the superficiality of doctrines, which belongs to man's natural life and is part of man's oldness. If every Christian was willing to be dealt with and to leave the natural things and the old creation behind, and if every one of them was willing to live in the reality of the Body of Christ, there would be no more divisions. May the Lord be merciful to us to see what the Body of Christ is. May the work of the cross usher us into the Body of Christ.

CHAPTER THREE

THE DIFFERENCE BETWEEN
BEING A BELIEVER AND BEING A MEMBER

Scripture Reading: Eph. 3:3-6; 4:15-16; Col. 3:10-11; Rom. 12:4-5; 1 Cor. 12:4-16, 20, 26

In the last two messages we saw that the church is the corporate Christ, and we saw also that in order to know the Body of Christ, we have to deal with our natural life.

THE BODY OF CHRIST BEING THE EXPRESSION OF CHRIST

What is the Body of Christ? The Body of Christ is the continuation of Christ's life on earth. When He came to the earth and lived on earth, He expressed Himself through a body. Today He still requires a body to express Himself. Just as a man needs a body to express all that he is, Christ needs a body to express Himself. The function of the Body is to be the full expression of Christ. We cannot manifest our personality through any one member of our body—the ears, mouth, eyes, hands, or feet—alone. Similarly, Christ cannot manifest His personality through any one member of His Body. It takes His whole Body to manifest Him. We must see that everything of Christ is expressed through His Body. This is not all. The Body of Christ is the extension and continuation of Christ on earth. He spent more than thirty years on earth to reveal Himself. He did this as the individual Christ. Today He is revealing Himself through the church. This is the corporate Christ. Formerly, Christ was expressed individually; now He is expressed corporately.

THE BODY OF CHRIST BEING
THE CORPORATE VESSEL TO FULFILL GOD'S PLAN

God is after a corporate vessel, not individual vessels. He

is not choosing a few zealous, consecrated ones to work for Him individually. Individual vessels cannot fulfill God's goal and plan. God has chosen the church, and He is after the church. Only the church as the corporate Christ can fulfill God's goal and plan.

Consider our human body. No member of our body can act independently. It is impossible for a body to depend on one hand or one leg. However, if the body loses a member, it will not be complete. The Body of Christ is composed of all the believers. Every believer is a member in the Body of Christ, and every believer is indispensable.

The Body of Christ is a reality. The church life is also a reality. The Word of God does not say the church is *like* the Body of Christ; it says the church *is* the Body of Christ. Nothing external can become part of our physical bodies. We may clothe our bodies, but the clothes do not become part of our bodies. Nothing that is of us can ever become part of the Body of Christ, because "Christ is all and in all" in the Body (Col. 3:11). Anything in us that is not a part of Christ frustrates our inward knowledge of the Body of Christ. Sin hinders us from seeing Christ, and the natural life hinders us from seeing the Body. We all must see our position in the Body of Christ. If we truly see our position in the Body, it will be as though we were saved a second time.

The Adamic life is individualistic and independent. Even though everyone in Adam shares the same life, there is no fellowship among them. We all commit sin, yet we each take our own way. Everyone in Adam lives as separate individuals. In Christ everything that is individualistic is ruled out. If we want to know the Body life, we need deliverance not only from our sinful life and our natural life, but also from our individualistic life. All individual elements must go because nothing that is individualistic can reach God's goal.

THE DIFFERENCE BETWEEN
BEING A MEMBER AND BEING A CHRISTIAN

The New Testament shows us that there is a difference between being a member and being a Christian. Being a Christian is something individualistic, whereas being a member is something corporate. Being a Christian is something one does for himself, whereas being a member is something for the Body. In the Bible there are many terms with opposite meanings, such as purity and uncleanness, holiness and commonness, victory and defeat, the Spirit and the flesh, Christ and Satan, the kingdom and the world, and glory and shame. All these are opposites. In the same way, the Body is in opposition to the individual. Just as the Father is versus the world, the Spirit is versus the flesh, and the Lord is versus the devil, so also is the Body versus the individual. Once a man sees the Body of Christ, he is free from individualism. He will no longer live for himself but for the Body. Once I am delivered from individualism, I am spontaneously in the Body.

The Body of Christ is not a doctrine; it is a realm. It is not a teaching, but a life. Many Christians seek to teach the truth of the Body, but few know the life of the Body. The Body of Christ is an experience in a totally different realm. A man can know the book of Romans without being justified. Similarly, a man can know the book of Ephesians without seeing the Body of Christ. We do not need knowledge; rather, we need revelation to know the reality of the Body of Christ and to enter the realm of the Body. Only a revelation from God will usher us into the realm of the Body, and only then will the Body of Christ become our experience.

In Acts 2 it seems as if Peter was preaching the gospel alone and that three thousand people were saved through him. But we must remember that the other eleven apostles were standing beside him. The Body of Christ was preaching the gospel; it was not the preaching of an individual. If we have the view of the Body, we will see that individualism will not bring us anywhere.

If we realize that a Christian is nothing more than a member, we will no longer be proud. Everything depends on our seeing. Those who see that they are members will surely treasure the Body and honor the other members. They will not see just their own virtues; they will readily see others as being better than themselves.

Every member has a function, and all the functions are

for the Body. The function of one member is the function of
the whole Body. When one member does something, the whole
Body does it. When the mouth speaks, the whole body is
speaking. When the hands work, the whole body is working.
When the legs walk, the whole body is walking. We cannot
divide the members from the body. Therefore, the movement
of the members of the Body must be focused around the Body.
Everything that the members do should be for the Body.
Ephesians 4 says that the Body is growing into a full-grown
man. It does not say that individuals are growing into
full-grown men. In chapter three the ability to know the love
of Christ and to apprehend the Lord's breadth, length, height,
and depth is with all the saints. No one can know or
apprehend by himself. An individual does not have the time
or the capacity to experience the love of Christ in that kind
of way.

First Corinthians 12:14 through 36 speaks of two erroneous
concepts that members may have: (1) "Because I am not...I
am not of the body" (v. 15). This is to despise oneself and
covet the work of others. (2) "I have no need of you" (v. 21).
This is to be proud of oneself, thinking that one man can be
all-inclusive, and despising others. Both concepts are harmful
to the Body. We should not imitate other members or be
covetous of other members. In this way we will not become
discouraged and give up when we find that we cannot be like
others. At the same time, we should not despise other
members, thinking that we are better and more useful.

THE CONSCIOUSNESS OF THE BODY

In the church life, we should learn to have the consciousness
of the Body. When we are at odds with the brothers and sisters,
it means that we are surely at odds with God. Some Christians
are like butterflies; they act independently. Others are like
bees; they live and move together. The butterfly flies from
flower to flower, going its own sweet way; but the bee works
for the hive. The butterfly lives and works individually, but
the bee has a body-consciousness. We should all be like bees,
having the consciousness of the Body so that we can live
together with other members in the Body of Christ. Wherever

there is Body-revelation, there is Body-consciousness, and wherever there is Body-consciousness, individual thought and action are automatically ruled out. Seeing Christ results in deliverance from sin; seeing the Body results in deliverance from individualism. Seeing the Body and deliverance from individualism are not two things but one. As soon as we see the Body, our life and work as individuals cease. It is not a matter of changing our attitude or conduct; revelation does the work. We cannot enter the realm of the Body by anything other than seeing. A real inward seeing settles the whole problem.

CHAPTER FOUR

THE SUPPLY OF THE BODY

Scripture Reading: Eph. 3:3-6; 2:15; Col. 3:10-11; 1 Cor. 12:20-21; Rom. 12:3-6

THE NEED FOR THE SUPPLY OF THE BODY

Every Christian should know that he is only a member. If he does not have the other members, he will not survive. In the Body all the members must be joined together before they can become the Body. All the members in the Body are related to one another, and they cannot be separated from one another. Between the members there must be a mutual supply and a mutual relatedness. Only then can the members survive. If a Christian lives an independent life, sooner or later he will weaken and dry up. If I am an ear, I cannot see and neither should I expect to see by myself. The whole body is dependent upon the eyes for sight, and no amount of prayer will give sight to the other members. If I am an ear, what should I do if I want to see something? I should go to the eyes—a brother or sister who sees—and ask for help. In order to go on with the Lord, we must recognize His supply for us in the Body and avail ourselves of it. The whole Body is built up through the interdependence among the members.

When I was in Southeast Asia, I had a talk with some brothers and sisters. Someone asked, "Why am I not living as before? I have not committed any particular sins that I know of, and I have not disobeyed the Lord in any way. I have not taken back my consecration or changed my mind about the money I have offered to the Lord. Outwardly, there does not seem to be any change in my spiritual condition. But why I am not the same as before? I seem to have lost the joy and the vitality that I once had." I answered, "The reason is that you have lived in your self for too long. You have to get into the Body life." In order for a member to live a normal life, he must receive the supply from the other members. If a man is not living in the Body of Christ, he will not receive the Body's supply. No member can say that he does not need the other members. No member may detach himself from other members to live alone.

Romans 12:3 says, "Not to think more highly of himself than he ought to think." We should not think too highly of ourselves, and we should not think that others are inferior. We should not despise and reject other members of the Body. Peter thought that the other members would fall and fail but that he would not. But when the test came, he failed just the same as everyone else. Those who think highly of themselves and despise other members will end up in trouble sooner or later. In the Body of Christ everyone is a member and nothing more than a member. Hence, no member can live without the other members, much less despise them.

THE INTERCESSION OF THE MEMBERS

Many of us have the experience that when we are dry and have no way to go on, we need other brothers and sisters to intercede for us before we can get through. Once I was sick for one hundred seventy-six days. I prayed for my own sickness every day, but it did not work. When I became exhausted, I asked a brother whom I did not think too highly of to pray for me. Amazingly, I received help from his intercession, and my condition became better within a short period of time. Brother Holz is known for his prayer life. When he was a missionary in China, he often asked a young brother to pray with him. Even if the young brother had nothing to say, it was still a help to him when the young brother sat in the room. Brothers and sisters, please remember that this is the supply of the Body. The supply of the Body of Christ is a reality. You cannot get through in many things no matter how much you struggle. But once you give the matter to the Body, the problem is solved. This is the supply of the Body of Christ.

In the years after 1930, many places in China experienced

the outpouring of the Holy Spirit, especially around Shantung province. At that time I had been saved for about ten years. I desired to have the outpouring, but I could not experience it. Later I went to Chefoo and asked the brothers and sisters there to pray for me. Not long afterwards, I received the outpouring. There was a brother in England who had the knowledge of victory in Christ, but he was unable to overcome a certain sin. A few brothers and I prayed for him, and he overcame. I can mention dozens of examples which show the effect of the Body's intercession. The prayer of the Body renders the life supply to members in need. God dispenses the life supply to His members through many other members. If the finger wants the supply of the blood, it has to receive it through the shoulder and the arm. Similarly, as members in the Body, we receive our supply through the other members. Therefore, it is foolish to try to separate ourselves from the other members.

LIVING IN THE BODY OF CHRIST

What are the eyes, ears, hands, and feet? They are Christ Himself. The Head is Christ, and the Body is also Christ. Each member is a part of the life of Christ. If I refuse the help of my fellow-members, I am refusing the help of Christ. If I am not willing to acknowledge my need of them, I am not willing to acknowledge my need of Christ. Just as I cannot be independent from the Head, I cannot be independent from the Body. Individualism is hateful in the sight of God. What I do not know, another member of the Body will know; what I cannot see, another member of the Body will see; what I cannot do, another member of the Body will do. Therefore, I must allow the other members of the Body to minister to my needs. We must avail ourselves constantly of the fellowship of the Body, for it is our very life.

In the Old Testament, being out of the fellowship was the most severe punishment that could be visited upon the children of Israel. They "shall be cut off from his people." This is very serious. If it were God's intention for us to live as individuals, we could progress perfectly well apart from one another. However, He has made us members of His Body; therefore, we cannot possibly grow apart from one another.

We have to see the reality of the supply in the Body of Christ, and we have to learn to live in the Body and to receive the supply in the Body. In the Old Testament the lampstand was placed in the sanctuary. In order for a man to see light, he had to enter the sanctuary. In the New Testament the sanctuary is the church. If a man wants to see light, he has to come to the church. In the church meetings and among the brothers and sisters, God's light is much stronger than in individuals. Today God's sanctuary is the church; God Himself dwells in the church. Hence, His light is in the church. A man can only see light if he comes to the church. Everything that Christ has is in His Body. He is a foolish man who claims that he can be a Christian alone. Sooner or later, all individual Christians will dry up. As long as we live in the Body, we will receive the supply of the Body, no matter what our condition is. Every member should learn to treasure the supply of the Body and to treasure every member. We must all learn to live in the Body, that is, we must all learn to live in the supply of the Body.

CHAPTER FIVE

THE PROTECTION, LIMITATION, AND MINISTRY OF THE BODY

Scripture Reading: Eph. 3:3-6; 2:15

THE PROTECTION OF THE BODY

We have seen that the church is the Body of Christ. This Body renders supply to every member of the Body. Furthermore, this Body also renders protection to every member. This is especially important when it comes to the matter of spiritual warfare. Ephesians is a book that deals specifically with the Body of Christ. In chapter six we see that spiritual warfare is something that is related to the church, not to individuals. It is the plural *you* that must put on the whole armor of God, not the singular *you*. Satan is not afraid of individuals. He is afraid of the church. "Upon this rock I will build My church, and the gates of Hades shall not prevail against it" (Matt. 16:18). We must meet the devil on the ground of the Body. Even in our private prayers we should stand by faith on the ground of the Body. Many Christians fall before the foe because they stand alone. In fact, if we stand alone, we invite Satan's attack.

We must remember that the spiritual armor is for the church, not for individuals. The Body of Christ puts on the whole armor of God. In the Body every member has its specialty, and all these specialties combined together form the whole armor of God. If a brother has faith, he has the shield of faith. If another brother has the word of God, he has the sword of the Spirit. The whole armor of God is the totality of all the specialties of the members. Hence, the whole armor is for the whole church, not for individuals. Spiritual warfare is an integrated warfare of all the members; it is not the isolated warfare of individuals. A single tree can be blown down easily, but a whole forest cannot be blown down easily. Satan likes to pick out those who are without any covering as the objects of his attacks. He looks for men who are alone and isolated. Whoever is under the protection of the Body is sheltered. One function of the Body of Christ is to protect all the members. We need the covering of the Body; otherwise, we will be constantly exposed to the enemy. An isolated individual is also prone to be deceived, so we need the covering of the Body for this as well. We should consult constantly with our fellow- believers. We must not only acknowledge the need for the Body in a general way, but we should also go to our brothers and sisters in a specific way and ask for help.

The Body of Christ is a reality; it is not a doctrine or a theory. The protection of the Body is also a reality and not a doctrine. Immediately after I was saved, I read in the Bible about bearing the cross. I thought that if I memorized the verses on this subject, I would be bearing the cross and that if I forgot the verses, I would not be bearing the cross. Later, I found out that bearing the cross has nothing to do with our memory. Our memory merely retains the doctrine. If the Lord's word is life to us, nothing will affect our bearing of the cross. It does not matter whether or not we remember the word, because if the word is life to us, it has already become a law of life in us and is no longer just an outward legal ordinance to us. The same is true with the Body of Christ—it is a law of life. Once we experience this life, we are under the operation of this law of life, and we discover that the protection of the Body is a reality and not an outward law.

Soldiers hide in the trenches for their protection in physical warfare. They cannot expose their heads; to do so is dangerous. This is also true in spiritual warfare. No member should be alone, and no member should expose his head. We are merely members in the Body, and we need the protection of the brothers and sisters. When Moses lifted up his hands to pray for the Israelites, he needed the help of Aaron and Hur. With their help the Israelites prevailed over the Amalekites. If a man as strong as Moses needed the help of his brothers, how much more do we need the help of our brothers? Many people do things without consulting and praying with the brothers and sisters. They are ignorant of the protection of the Body, and the result is nothing but failure. We all must see the reality of the Body's protection, hide under its protection, and accept its safeguard.

This is the difference between one who has revelation of the Body and one who does not: The one who knows the Body merely as a truth may seek the counsel and covering of the Body, but he will do it as a matter of policy, not as a matter of life. When he thinks of it he will do it, but he can also forget about it. The one who has seen the Body as a reality and has entered experientially into the realm of the Body has no possibility of forgetting. His acting by the Body-principle is something spontaneous because it is his life.

THE LIMITATION OF THE BODY

If you are simply a believer, you can act as you please, but if you are a member of the Body, then you must allow yourself to be limited by the other members. Here we find the necessity of the cross. The cross leads to the Body, and the cross operates in the sphere of the Body. If I am quick and another is slow, I must not insist on keeping my own pace; I must allow myself to be limited by the slow member. If I am a prophet, then I must give way to the evangelist when it comes to the matter of preaching to the unsaved. I should not feel the need to preach just because I have the gift of prophecy. "To each one of us grace was given according to the measure of the gift of Christ" (Eph. 4:7). It is essential for the development of the Body that we each recognize our measure and not go beyond it. This is a basic requirement for the growth of the Body.

The Body of Christ is not only a protection to the members but a limitation to all the members. Every Christian is but one member in the Body of Christ and must accept the limitation of the Body. We should not allow ourselves to go our own way; rather, we should learn to be blended with other brothers and sisters. Individual dispositions and peculiarities have no place in the church. Every member should honor the talents of others and be faithful to his own. Moreover, every member should know his own capacity and not consider himself more highly than he should. If everyone does this, there will be no jealousy, ambition, or craving to do what others can do. In 2 Corinthians 10:14 Paul said, "For we are not extending ourselves beyond our bounds, as if we did not reach you." Yet many people have not seen their own capacity. As a result they overstep their boundaries. Those who over-step their boundaries are trampling others under their feet; they are kicking others, pressing upon others, and usurping the portion of other members. If members behave this way in the church, some will begin to monopolize while others will withdraw, and the result will be a loss to the church. We should not behave in this way. We should turn back and take our place in the Body and be limited by the Body. If we do this, the Body will be spared from damage.

THE MINISTRY OF THE BODY

The fellowship in the Body involves not only receiving help from other members but also giving help to other members. The functioning of the Body is mutual. Mutuality is the characteristic of the Body. Even when there is ministry from the pulpit, the ministry should never be one-sided. The pulpit needs the help of the congregation just as the congregation needs the help of the pulpit. Merely being a listener or an onlooker is contrary to the life of the Body. Every Christian should have a part in the meeting and render supply to other members. This kind of supply is the ministry of the members and the function of the members. It is also the fellowship of life. No member should cut himself off from this fellowship. If you stop this fellowship, life will stop flowing, and you will become a burden to the Body. If a person thinks that he does not need to say anything, and that he will be approved of and not cause any trouble as long as he simply, quietly, and politely receives from others, he does not know what the Body of Christ is. Every member has to render supply to the Body and fellowship and function in the Body. This is a law of the Body. In the physical body no member can cease functioning without there being a loss to the whole body. This is also true in the Body of Christ.

In the church meeting every member should function according to the leading of the Holy Spirit. First Corinthians 14:26 says, "What then, brothers? Whenever you come together, each one has a psalm, has a teaching, has a revelation... Let all things be done for building up." In spite of this, many people come to the meetings as spectators. They are a heavy burden to the Body. The Lord told the Pharisees that if His disciples did not rejoice and praise God with great shouting, the rocks would cry out. It is abnormal to not function in the meeting, and this is not pleasing to the Lord. Every time you come to a meeting, you should enter into the fellowship. With every believer, there should be the flow of life. If you do not fellowship, you hinder God's life and kill the meeting. I have often asked those who come to the bread-breaking meeting whether they are coming as spectators or whether they are coming for fellowship. Anyone who hinders God's life is not only bringing death to the meeting but also bringing death upon himself. What do you contribute to your fellow members when the church gathers together?

If a member fails to function, not only do the other members suffer loss, but the member himself is impoverished. I am enriched by giving to others. When I quench others' thirst, my own thirst is quenched. This is like the Lord's experience with the woman in John 4. The Lord was thirsty, but His own thirst was satisfied when He took care of the spiritual thirst of the woman. When His disciples brought Him food, He said, "I have food to eat that you do not know about" (v. 32). He was ministered to by ministering to another. Whenever we try to satisfy ourselves, we end up being hungry. But whenever we satisfy others, we are fed. When we bear the burdens of others, our own burden becomes light.

Many people complain that this or that meeting is not good. They do not realize the kind of attitude that they have brought to the meeting. Whenever we stop functioning, we frustrate God's life. When we come to the meeting, we have to open our mouth, release life, and participate in the Body ministry. Once I was preaching in a place, and the meeting was very dead. But one of the sisters rendered a great help by responding to my words. She kept saying "amen" to my speaking and responded with much expression on her face, indicating that she was taking in my words. Because of her response, I was released and God's word was also released.

May the Lord show us that we all have a share in the meeting. It is not enough for us to speak about the Body; we have to express the Body in our living. The Body of Christ is not a doctrine; it is a reality in life. God wants us to enter into the Body life, not to have the doctrine of the Body. We have received the life of the Body, not a doctrine about the Body. Martin Luther did not receive the doctrine of justification by faith but the life of justification by faith. As a consequence his ministry was powerful. The justification that he spoke of was not a doctrine but a reality in life. Today we all must receive the revelation of the reality of the Body and enter into the life of the Body. Then we will see that we are members of the Body of Christ, that we need the protection and limitation of the Body, and that we need to function in the Body and supply other members so that the life of the Body will flow in an unhindered way.

CHAPTER SIX

AUTHORITY IN THE BODY

Scripture Reading: Eph. 1:22; 2:15; 3:3-6; 4:15-16; Col. 2:19; 3:10-11

THE AUTHORITY OF THE BODY RESTING IN THE HEAD

The Bible emphatically tells us that Christ is the Head. One day God will head up everything in the universe under Christ. Today the universe has not come under the headship of Christ yet, and everything is in a state of confusion. But one day God will head up everything under the headship of Christ. God ordained that Christ should exercise headship over all things, but today that headship must first be exercised in the church, and then through the church the headship will be exercised over all things. Today Christ is the Head of the church. Eventually, He will be the Head over all things. The church is God's means of enlarging Christ, and this enlargement will go on until He fills the entire universe. The church is "the fullness of the One who fills all in all" (Eph. 1:23). If the headship of Christ is not established in the church, it cannot be established in the universe.

What do Christ being the Head of the church and the church being the Body of Christ mean? They mean that all authority is in Him. All authority is in Him because all life is in Him. The whole Body is consummated in Him; He is the fountainhead of the life of the Body. The Body has no life of its own. "God gave to us eternal life and this life is in His Son" (1 John 5:11). Even after eternal life is given to us, it still rests in His Son. The Son does not part with it; He retains it in Himself. "He who has the Son has the life" (v. 12). This verse does not say, "He who has the life has the life." We do not possess life as life; only by possessing the Son do we have life. A Christian receives his life from the Lord. Yet this life can never be separated from the Lord. A believer is related not just to life. By being related to this life, a believer is related to the Son of God. This life makes us members of the Body of Christ. This life relationship rules out the possibility of being separated from the Head, because our life is derived from the Head. The flow of life in us continually depends upon our relationship to the Son. As soon as there is any obstruction in our fellowship with Him, the life in us is immediately blocked. He is the Head of the Body, and life can flow freely to us only when He is in full control.

THE MEMBERS' PLACE BEING TO SUBMIT TO THE AUTHORITY OF THE HEAD

The power of our existence is derived from Christ. This is why we cannot do anything independently. Only the Lord is our Head, and only He has the authority to direct the moves of the members of His Body. In this age of lawlessness, any suggestion of the need of authority is unwelcome; but if we are to understand and enter into the life of the Body, we must know the authority of the Head. My hand can do nothing without direction from the head. The head must command if the members are to move. Christ is the life of the Body, and Christ is also the authority in the Body. All the moves of the members of His Body must be under the direction of the Head. For Christ to be the Head means that He has the authority in the Body. We are not the head, and we do not have the authority. The only thing we should do is submit to the authority of the Lord. If we seek to know the life of the Body, a question will immediately arise: Do we bow to the absolute authority of the Lord? We will be challenged at the outset by the headship of Christ. We cannot say, "But..." We cannot say, "I think..." We can only bow to His sovereignty. We need to realize that if we are going to be members of the Body, we cannot be the Head. We cannot dictate, choose, or even desire. The Bible says that we should follow the Lord. What does it mean to follow the Lord? Following means coming after. The Lord is the One who decides our pathway. We do not have any ground for our own choice. The Body's only duty toward the

Head is obedience and submission without any opinion, idea, or proposal. In the Body of Christ, no individual's idea or proposal counts; all these have to be cast down. We should only submit to the authority of the Head. We should just listen to His command and do as He says.

An acceptance of Christ as Head involves a repudiation of all other heads. Christ alone is the Head of the Body; no one else can be the head. You cannot be the head, nor can anyone in the church be the head, because there can only be one Head in the Body; there cannot be two heads. Only Christ is the Head. Therefore, all of us have to obey Christ. Today we see many human methods and ordinances abounding in the church. How wrong this is! Human plans and human decisions are against the headship of Christ. If Christ is my Head, then I will not dare to please myself or others; I must seek to please Him alone. "God has made Him both Lord and Christ" (Acts 2:36). Note that God has not set up Christ as Savior but as Lord. Paul first saw Christ as Lord and then as Savior. When he was apprehended on the road to Damascus, his first question was, "Who are You, *Lord?*" (9:5). Only Christ is the Head in the church; there is no other head. If we desire to live in the Body of Christ, we have to learn to submit to the authority of our Lord Jesus. Anyone who cannot submit, who always expresses his opinions and proposals, and who insists on being the head has never seen the Body. Once a man realizes that he is a member in the Body, there will surely be a feeling of submission in him because submission is a law of the Body.

HOLDING THE HEAD

Paul spoke of "holding the Head, out from whom all the Body, being richly supplied and knit together by means of the joints and sinews, grows with the growth of God" (Col. 2:19). Since Christ is the Head of the Body, we have to hold the Head. Holding the Head is acknowledging that only Christ is the Head; it is coming absolutely under His authority. We can be joined to the brothers and sisters only when we hold the Head. The members of the Body are fitted together and able to live the Body life through holding the

Head. Our relationship to the Head determines our relationship to the other members. All the questions regarding our relationship with the brothers and sisters can only be solved when we come under the absolute authority of the Lord. Unless we recognize the headship of Christ in the Body, we will never have a perfect fellowship with the other members, because it is our common relationship to Him that causes us to be related to one another. We may look different outwardly, but the Christ within us is the same. This is why we can fellowship with one another and be one with each other. Apart from Christ, we have no means of fellowship. When we do not hold the Head, our fellowship becomes invalid. The basis of our fellowship is our mutual holding of the Head. When we all hold the Head, we will hold to one another, and our relationship with the Body will be proper.

If we hold the Head, we cannot have a special relationship, feeling, or fellowship with any individual or group of individuals. There is no room for our own preferences in the Body. We have no direct communion one with another; it is all through the Head. For instance, when my left hand hurts, my right hand comes to its aid immediately. The right hand does this because both the left hand and the right hand are under the direction of the head. The mutual relationship of the members passes through the Head first. What does it mean to form parties? Forming parties means that a few Christians have a direct relationship with one another and are detached from the authority of the Head. They communicate with each other directly, but their communication has not passed through the Head. They have a special relationship with one another, but their relationship has not passed through the Head.

We must not move in relation to another member except under the direction of the Lord. If He asks us to do something for a fellow member and the fellow member does not appreciate it, we do not need to worry since all of our dealings are with the Head. If we hold the Head, getting all our direction from Him and doing all as unto Him, we do not need to worry about the consequences.

If we hold the Head, we cannot have different interpretations of Scripture. Differences arise when someone is not holding the Head, because He cannot possibly say one thing to one member and something else to another. If differences arise, we must not try to straighten them out by discussion; rather, we should just recognize Christ as the Head. In the church we all must hold the Head, whether it involves the understanding of the truth, the handling of business, or any other matter. Christ is the unique authority in the Body. The place of all the members is to hold the Head and to acknowledge Him as the unique and supreme authority in all things. If we let the cross deal with our natural life, we will find no difficulty in our relationship with the fellow members of the Body.

Chapter Seven

THE ANOINTING OF THE BODY

Scripture Reading: 1 John 2:27; Luke 3:22; 4:18; Eph. 4:1-10, 30-32; Psa. 133

The Bible shows us that God's anointing is only for the One who has totally satisfied God's heart—His Son, Christ. If this is so, why does the Body receive the anointing? Psalm 133 shows us that the fine oil was poured on Aaron's head and ran down upon his beard to the hem of his garments. When a man is anointed, the oil is poured on the head of the anointed, not on the whole body. Yet after the oil is poured, it runs downward and eventually flows to the whole body. Because the Head is Christ, the Anointed One, the Body is also Christ. Christ is God's Anointed. The church is His Body. When Christ was anointed, the whole Body was anointed with Him. Christ is the great Anointed One, while the members are the little anointed ones. Yet we are not anointed separately; we were anointed in His Body, that is, in Christ, when He was anointed. It is impossible for us to be anointed in ourselves, because the Bible says, "Upon man's flesh shall it not be poured" (Exo. 30:32). We are anointed in Christ.

THE CONDITION FOR THE ANOINTING BEING THE BURIAL OF THE NATURAL MAN

Luke 3:22 tells us what happened after the Lord was baptized in the river Jordan. "The Holy Spirit descended in bodily form as a dove upon Him. And a voice came out of heaven: You are My Son, the Beloved; in You I have found My delight." Luke 4:18 says, "The Spirit of the Lord is upon Me, because He has anointed Me to announce the gospel to the poor." From these verses we see that the Lord was anointed with the Holy Spirit when He came out of the water of baptism at the Jordan River. Genesis 8 records that after the flood, Noah opened the window of the ark and sent out a dove. However, the dove could not find any place to rest because the whole earth was filled with water, and it returned back to the ark. (The passage of Noah's ark through the deluge is a type of baptism.) At the time of Christ's baptism, the Spirit of God descended upon Him like a dove. This signifies that at the time of Christ's baptism, He received the anointing of the Holy Spirit. In the same way, when we were baptized, we also received the anointing of the Spirit.

Baptism signifies that everything of the old, natural man is buried. For the anointing to come after baptism means that in order for us to receive the anointing of the Holy Spirit, our flesh must first be buried. Only that which is of the Lord can rise up after baptism because anything that belongs to the believers themselves is only qualified for burial. Anything that can rise up after burial has to be something in resurrection. It can rise up because Christ is in it. When we are baptized in Christ, we pass through death, burial, and resurrection with Him. Hence, when He was anointed, we were anointed also. We are crucified, buried, resurrected, and anointed together with Him.

THE FUNCTION OF THE ANOINTING

The anointing is so precious because grace flows from the Head to the Body by means of the anointing. The function of the anointing is to maintain the link between the Head and the Body, as well as the link between all the members. The anointing is the operation of the Holy Spirit within man. The relationship between the Holy Spirit, Christ, and the church can be compared to the nerves in the human body. The nerves direct and coordinate all the members of the body. The head communicates and directs all the members through the nerves, and through the nerves all the members are related one to another as well. All the members in the body move according to the direction of the nerves. Submitting to the nerves is submitting to the head. Likewise, in the spiritual Body the Holy Spirit carries the thoughts of the Head to all the members. As members of the Body of Christ, we have to yield to the authority of the Holy Spirit. When we yield to the authority of the Holy Spirit, we are yielding to the Head. When we grieve the Spirit, we frustrate our relationship with the Head. We hold the Head by simply yielding to the Spirit.

THE TEACHING OF THE ANOINTING

In the Bible the Holy Spirit is symbolized by many things, such as the wind, the living water, and the fire. At the same time, the Holy Spirit is also life, power, etc. However, 1 John 2:27 is particularly sweet in its description of the Holy Spirit as the anointing. This is the teaching of the Holy Spirit. The Holy Spirit teaches by the anointing. We do not know the will of God by studying and weighing the pros and cons of a particular matter. We know the will of God by the teaching of the anointing. The Holy Spirit communicates the mind of Christ to us. It is not necessary to continually ask, "Is this the will of God?" "We *have* the mind of Christ" (1 Cor. 2:16). When the Head wishes a member of the Body to move, He intimates it through the anointing, and as we yield to the anointing, life flows freely from the Head. If we resist the anointing, the relationship with the Head is interfered with and the flow of life stops. Many believers miss the leading of the Lord because they are not under the Head. The anointing does not come directly upon the Body but upon the Head. Believers can receive the anointing which flows from the Head to the Body only when they are directly under the Head.

The anointing is something very fine and soothing. The teaching of the Holy Spirit is not something rough or wild. It does not blow on us like the wind or burn us like fire. Rather, it anoints us like oil. This is how the Holy Spirit teaches us. Wherever there is the oil, there is the work of God. His work does not depend on words, biblical interpretations, reasons, judgments concerning right and wrong, etc. God's work and leading within us come by way of a kind of inner sense of life. This sense of life is the anointing of the Spirit. The Head does not use external means to control the Body. "The life was the light of men" (John 1:4). In seeking to know the will of God, we cannot arrive at it by asking, "Is this right or wrong?" Rather, we should ask, "Do I have life regarding this?" If we feel dead inside, then there is no anointing, and if we act without the anointing, we are acting without the authority of the Head. For example, sometimes we may want to visit someone, but we feel cold and indifferent within. As far as doctrines, human affections, or biblical principles are concerned, we should visit him. But the more we resolve to go, the colder we become. This means that the Spirit is telling us not to go. At another time, we may visit someone and feel as if we are under some kind of sweet anointing; everything is soothing and comfortable. This is the teaching that comes from the Spirit's anointing. The more we go along with this anointing, the stronger we will be, and the more there will be an "amen" within.

The teaching of the anointing of the Spirit has nothing to do with right or wrong, what should or should not be done, or what is true or false. It is an inner feeling of life. Many people still work according to the principle of the tree of the knowledge of good and evil, the tree from which Adam ate. This is to walk according to the principle of right and wrong; however, God's work in Christ is a matter of life. It is a matter of the anointing of the Spirit. Where the anointing is, there is life. As long as one has the anointing and the life, everything is right and according to God's desire. Those who are clever and acquainted with Bible doctrines are not necessarily more familiar with God's work. Sometimes a brother or sister from the rural countryside may know more about God's work. They do not have knowledge, but they have life. If this were not God's way, He would be very unfair. Illiterate country folk would be doomed because they would not have the mental knowledge and would be unable to know God's will. But our God is not a respecter of persons. Whether or not we have the mental knowledge and whether we are clever or slow, the teaching of the anointing still abides in us. As long as we walk according to the inner anointing of the Spirit, we will know God's will and be acquainted with God's work.

THE ANOINTING AND THE LAW

In the Old Testament men had God's word—the law. In the New Testament, men also have God's word. But if this word does not have the Spirit's anointing behind it, it is also a law. The Lord Jesus presented God's word, but that word was spirit and life. The apostles also presented God's word, and that word was also spirit and life. But when the Pharisees presented God's word, there was no anointing of the Spirit, and that word became dead laws. Many people practice baptism, the laying on of hands, and head covering merely according to the instructions of the Bible. These things are the law to them. If a man acts merely according to the letter of the Bible, he is a disciple of Moses and not a Christian. A Christian has the Lord's anointing on him. In the Body of Christ, there is no law; there is only the Lord's anointing. Hence, in order for us to live in the Body of Christ, we have to walk according to the Spirit's anointing, not according to the letter of the law. We must do everything according to the anointing of the Spirit. This is walking according to the teaching of the Spirit.

THE WAY TO BE ANOINTED

How do we receive the anointing? Psalm 133 is the key passage in the Old Testament concerning the anointing. We should realize that Psalms 120 through 134 are songs of ascent. These are the songs the Israelites sang three times a year when they ascended from different places to meet the Lord in Zion in Jerusalem, the dwelling place of God. Although all the songs are different, they have one thing in common—they are all ascending songs. The people did not talk about economics, education, warfare, or politics. Their hearts were toward Zion, toward God, and they were going upward. Psalm 133:1 says, "Behold, how good and how pleasant it is / For brothers to dwell in unity!" This dwelling in unity is corporate; there is no barrier or separation. They have cast aside their disunity, jealousy, and hatred. This is like the fine oil that was poured on Aaron's head that ran down upon the beard to the hem of his garments. In this condition, they receive God's anointing. When the oil flows down, those who are under the head will spontaneously receive the oil. Psalm 133 is equivalent to Ephesians 4. When we are in the Body and are diligent to keep the oneness of the Spirit, we have the anointing of the Spirit. We have to come under the Head, and we have to live in the Body before we can receive the anointing. Many people do not receive any leading because they are not standing in the right place. They are not under the Head and have not submitted themselves to the authority of the Head. Neither are they in the Body. In order for us to receive the anointing, we must submit to the Head and live in the Body.

The believers' fellowship is based on Christ. We can fellowship with one another because Christ is the life of the Body and the Head of the Body. At the same time, the enjoyment of this fellowship is the Holy Spirit. The more we live in the fellowship of the Body, the more we enjoy the anointing of the Spirit. But there is a condition to this: We have to allow the cross to deal with our flesh and our natural life in a thorough way. Whether or not a believer can enjoy this fellowship depends on whether he has dealt with his natural life. Our natural flesh only deserves to die; it only deserves to be in ashes, to be on the cross. We cannot think by ourselves; we are not qualified to propose anything by ourselves. We must allow Christ to have the absolute sovereignty over everything. We must allow Him to be the Lord in an absolute way. If our natural life is dealt with by the cross and if we submit to the headship of Christ and live the Body life, we will have the Spirit's anointing and enjoy the fellowship of the Body.

CHAPTER EIGHT

THE ORDER OF THE BODY

Scripture Reading: Rom. 12:3-8; Eph. 4:9-16; Col. 2:19; 1 Cor. 11:29

THE MINISTRY OF THE MEMBERS

First Corinthians 12:18 says, "But now God has placed the members, each one of them, in the body, even as He willed." This shows that every member has a definite place, definite assignment, and definite position. Every member has a particular portion with which he serves the Body of Christ. The eyes see, the ears hear, and the nose smells. Each organ has its function, and each has its portion. The eyes serve the body by seeing. The ears serve the body by hearing. The nose serves the body by smelling. Each has its own responsibility, and none can replace another. Member A cannot be member B, and member B cannot be member C. Each member has his own characteristics, and each has his own capability. These characteristics and capabilities constitute the place, position, or ministry of each member.

The characteristics of a member are the ministry of that member, which is the supply it renders to the Body. The ministry of a member dictates his place and position in the Body. The portion of each member in the Body is not for himself, but for the whole Body. Our service in the Body of Christ is based on what we have received particularly from the Lord. The particular knowledge and experience we have acquired from the Lord become our supply to the Body. Yet many Christians have acquired only reeds—amounting to nothing but knowledge that they have heard and doctrines that they have studied. These are reed weapons; they are not the sword of the Spirit, and they will prove to be useless in time of need. One theologian despised his wife for not knowing the Bible, but when his son became ill, he could not remain calm. His wife, who had a much deeper knowledge of God, was more trusting, peaceful, and firm in her faith. Doctrines that are gained from study do not avail much. Only the life that comes from the Lord counts, and only that supplies the Body.

FUNCTIONING IN ORDER

We supply the Body with the life that we have received from Christ the Head. Yet when we function, we have to be proper and in order. Order in the Body is essential to growth and ministry. In the physical body, any dislocation or disproportionate growth of the members hinders its functioning. This is also true in the Body of Christ. In the meeting no one will stop you from speaking. But you have to speak according to your measure of faith and according to the leading of the Spirit. You have to know whether there is any overstepping in your speaking, and you have to know whether your speaking is too long. Many believers crave to be outstanding Christians and outstanding workers, but if some become overdeveloped, others will be underdeveloped. The result would not be the Body but a monstrosity; God's order in the church would be destroyed. When we truly come under the authority of the Head, He sets us in our special place in the Body and appoints us to our special function.

In the denominational organizations, leaders are selected according to background, social status, education, knowledge, intelligence, eloquence, or talent. But they may not have any revelation, faith, or experience in the Lord. They can only bring natural things to the church. They will not supply the Body; on the contrary, they will bring death to the Body. The ministry of the Body is not determined by natural things. A member functions in the Body according to what he has received from the Lord. It is according to the "measure of faith" (Rom. 12:3, 6). At the same time, it is according to God's assigned order. Therefore, we have to seek revelation and experience from Christ so that we can have something to supply the Body, and we have to know the order of the

Body, which is God's assigned pattern in the Body. We must be willing to be limited to our measure. As soon as we go beyond it, we go beyond the authority of the Head and move out from under the anointing. When we go beyond our measure, we interfere with the order of the Body. The Body of Christ is an organic life; it operates without any human arrangement. All the members must receive life from the Head and function in proper order. If our relationship with the Head is proper, we will keep our place in the Body spontaneously.

APOSTLES, PROPHETS, EVANGELISTS, SHEPHERDS AND TEACHERS

Ephesians 4:11 speaks of a group of people who are for the Body; they are God's gifts to the church, supplying Christ for the building up of the Body. We have to pay special attention to this group of members.

The apostles are the first gift that God has appointed in the Body of Christ. They are sent by God to represent the authority of the Head and to execute God's will on earth. Hence, in a church that is a proper testimony of the Body, all the believers should submit to the representative authority. In the Old Testament, Moses did not argue when Korah and his company repudiated Moses' authority as God's prophet. Instead, he referred the matter to God, who made it clear that touching the anointed of the Lord was the same as touching the Lord Himself, and that repudiating the authority of His prophet was the same as repudiating His authority. The result of such a touching and repudiation is death upon the offenders. God requires us to come directly under not only the authority of the Lord but also the authority of those who represent His authority in the Body. When the head orders the arm to move, the little finger must move with the arm. The arm illustrates representative authority. We must keep our position in the Body under the headship of Christ and under the authority of those in the Body to whom He has sovereignly given His authority. It is much easier to bow to the direct authority of God than to the authority of His representatives in the Body. Bowing to the authority of His representative takes meekness and humility. We cannot disregard God's order with impunity, as we see in Paul's letter to Corinth (1 Cor. 11:29-30). There is no room for individual thought or action in the Body of Christ. The Body moves under the control of the Head. Disobeying the law of the Body means weakness and death.

The prophets not only predict future events but also speak forth God's mind. They are those who are sent by God to His people to convey His mind. The greatest prophet in the Old Testament was Elijah, not Isaiah, because most of Isaiah's words were prophecies, whereas Elijah primarily conveyed God's mind. When a prophet receives a revelation from the Lord, he conveys God's mind to His people. A prophet is one who knows and declares God's mind, whereas a person who predicts merely foretells future events. In the Body there is a special group of ministers who know God's mind and who make it known to the Body. These ones are also the representative authority of the Head.

Evangelists make known the compassions of God in Christ, while shepherds and teachers make known God's riches in Christ and render others the supply through these riches. Each of these ministers is a "joint of the rich supply" (Eph. 4:16). They receive life from God and communicate it to the whole Body. Many Christians say, "I am in direct communication with the Source of supply; I can get everything for *myself* from the Head." Such an attitude is a repudiation of the authority of the Lord, who in His sovereignty has ordained that the members would be dependent not only on Him but also on one another.

How do these "joints of the rich supply" serve the Body? They must be those who have gone through special training under the Lord's hand and have been specially molded through the environment ordered by the Spirit; they have a history of knowing Christ. They are tried and tested and instructed by Christ, and they are qualified to transmit spiritual values. They have a secret history in tribulation, and the cross has wrought the things that they minister to the Body into them.

ELDERS

In addition, in the local assembly there are members who have the right to exercise authority. They are not merely *given* authority; they *have* authority. These are those who hold the office of elders. They occupy this position, not because they have been *made* elders, but because they *are* elders. Elders are manifested in a spontaneous way by the Holy Spirit; the only thing that man can do is identify and confirm. In a spiritual church the most spiritual members hold the office of elders; in a carnal church the office is held by those who have the best natural qualifications. When a man marries and has a son, he becomes a father. No one can be appointed to hold the office of a father. A man either *is* a father or *is not* a father; he cannot be *made* a father. Likewise, no one can be made an elder. He either is an elder or is not an elder. Elders are not elected through campaigns and elections; they are manifested in a spontaneous way through maturity in life. They should be those who are purer in heart and who are seeking for and growing in spiritual things. Their duty is to help others obey the Head. If a person is an elder, all that the church has to do is recognize what he is and allow him to function accordingly.

THE MAN BEING THE HEAD OF THE WOMAN

In God's arrangement, the man is the head of the woman. Therefore, sisters have no administrative power in the church. This does not mean, however, that any man can be the head of a woman; only those who are under Christ can be the head of the sisters. The covering of the sisters' heads indicates that they maintain the order in the Body, that they submit to Christ as well as to the authority of the Body.

Strictly speaking, there is no authority in the Body; all authority lies in the Head. The weakness of the so-called church today is that authority has become a matter of position, not of life. In the Body of Christ authority is a matter of life, not of position. If a member has authority, it is because that authority has been wrought into him already. He has passed through God's dealing, and authority has become life in him. God does not set up certain individuals to *act* as eyes, ears, mouth, hands, etc. He makes them these things by the operation of the cross. When they *are* these organs, they naturally function in that capacity. The whole issue rests on life. As long as we obey the life of the Body, which flows as the Body maintains its position under the absolute authority of the Head, there will be continuous and perfectly proportioned growth. Unless we are truly in the life of the Body, there cannot be increase in the measure of Christ.

Apostles and elders have no authority in themselves; they only have authority as they stand under the authority of the Lord. They exercise authority in the Body by representing the authority of the Head. If the apostles and elders have the mind of God, then they have the authority of God, for He only upholds that for which He Himself stands. Whatever He authorizes, He supports by His authority.

The life of the Body necessitates drastic dealings with the natural life. We must be broken before we will submit to the representative authority in the Body and be willing to minister and be ministered unto in our sovereignly ordained place. God cannot allow lawlessness to come into His church, because this makes the development of the Body impossible. He cannot allow any human head to raise itself, because this also hinders the development of the Body and denies the headship of Christ. Any desire on the part of a believer to exercise authority is contrary to the life of the Body. Christ alone is the Head, and we are all members one of another. If anyone claims to have a revelation of the Body yet is not in subjection to the authority of the Body or properly related to the other members, the claim is false. As soon as we truly see the Body, we will also see the need of obedience and mutual relatedness. Submission is one outstanding characteristic of those who are familiar with the life of the Body.

God has made definite arrangements and instituted order in the Body of Christ. We must be careful to discern the Body, as 1 Corinthians 11:29 charges us to do. We cannot be careless in the Body and make proposals lightly or overstep presumptuously. Every member must be in proper order and walk in an orderly way. Authority is ordained by the Lord; no one can be an authority in himself, and no one can elect others to be an authority. Authority comes from the Lord's arrangement and is for the Body life. We should be clear about our position in the Body and maintain our position. In the Body life, we all must walk according to the order in the Body.

CHAPTER NINE

THE PRINCIPLE OF THE BODY

Scripture Reading: Acts 6:6; 8:4-5, 12, 14-17; 9:3-6, 10-12, 17; 19:6; James 5:14-16; Matt. 18:15-16, 19-20; 1 Tim. 4:14; 5:22; 2 Tim. 1:6

THE APOSTLES' LAYING ON OF HANDS

There is an example in Acts 8 that shows us the principle of the Body. At that time the church in Jerusalem suffered great persecution, and except for the apostles, all the disciples were dispersed. Philip was not an apostle; he only took care of the distribution of food. But because he had life, he went down to Samaria and preached the gospel. Many believed and were baptized, and there was "much joy in that city" (v. 8). But there was a difference between these saved ones and the believers in Jerusalem. These saved ones did not have the Spirit upon them yet. Therefore, the apostles sent Peter and John as representatives to fill up the lack. They laid hands on the new converts, and the new converts received the Holy Spirit.

What is the significance of the laying on of hands? According to Leviticus, when a man offered a sacrifice, the offerer had to lay his hands on the offering. This means that the laying on of hands is a sign of identification. Many places in the New Testament speak of the laying on of hands. First Timothy 5:22 says, "Lay hands quickly on no man," lest, as Paul explained, we should "participate in others' sins." This shows once again that the laying on of hands signifies an identification. We have to be careful lest we "participate in others' sins." In the Old Testament, when kings or priests were appointed, there was the laying on of hands as well as the anointing upon the head. Hence, there are two main meanings of the laying on of hands: It puts the believers under the anointing of the Head, and it brings the believers into the fellowship of the Body.

The apostles are the representatives of God. They are also representative members in the Body of Christ. When Peter and John laid their hands on the believers in Samaria, their act brought those upon whom they laid hands under the authority of the Head and into the fellowship of the Body. This means that they were acknowledged as part of the Body. Once they were brought into the one Body and came under the one anointing, the Holy Spirit immediately fell upon them. If the saved ones in Samaria had received the Holy Spirit before the apostles arrived, Philip would have been able to boast that Peter and John had their work in Jerusalem while he had his work in Samaria. If this had been the case, the saved ones in Samaria would have become separate from the saved ones in Jerusalem. If some had claimed Peter for Jerusalem and others had claimed Philip for Samaria, the principle of the Body would have been broken. The events in Samaria show us that unless one submits to the Body, he cannot receive the anointing. We cannot have the anointing if we do not recognize the Body. The Holy Spirit is not given to individuals but to members of the Body. The apostles' laying on of hands brought the believers into the fellowship of the Body. Hence, the laying on of hands acknowledges that there is union, fellowship, and one Body. The Body is one; therefore, the members need to recognize their dependence not only on the Head but also on one another.

Hebrews 6:1-2 speaks of six items as "the word of the beginning." The laying on of hands is one of the six foundational matters of the Christian life. These six items can be divided into three groups. The first group includes repentance from dead works and faith in God. This is an inward attitude or action taken by one toward himself or toward God. The third group includes the resurrection of the dead and eternal judgment. These are teachings that have to do with things in the future. The second group includes baptism and the laying on of hands. These two items are outward testimonies. Baptism and the laying on of hands are two testimonies of the church that are essential for those who are to "be brought on to maturity." We have not neglected five of these items, but we have neglected one of them—the laying on of hands. Although the Bible does not clearly say that we must practice the laying on of hands, it does show us that at the time of the apostles, a man received the laying on of hands as soon as he was saved and baptized. By baptism we enter into Christ. By the laying on of hands we enter into the Body. Believers are put not only into Christ, but also into the Body of Christ. This is our proper position. We know that every believer should break bread on the Lord's Day. The breaking of bread refreshes our memory of the significance of baptism and the laying on of hands. By baptism we bear witness to the fact that we have put off ourselves and the world and entered into Christ. By the laying on of hands we bear witness to the fact that we have left the ground of being an individual and taken a stand on the ground of the Body. Henceforth, even if circumstances take us to a place of geographical isolation, we will not be alone, because the whole Body will be with us. If we suffer, all of the members will suffer with us, and we can count on them coming to our aid continually.

At the time of the laying on of hands, if the Holy Spirit gives prophetic prayer for the one who is being brought under the anointing, then the specific features set forth in prophecy will characterize the future life and ministry of that one. We have an illustration of this in the case of Timothy. When Paul and the elders laid hands on him, prophetic utterance was given, and Paul later exhorted Timothy to not neglect the gift imparted to him, but to fan it into flame (1 Tim. 1:18; 4:14; 2 Tim. 1:6). If we truly have a revelation of the Body, we must have the laying on of hands. It is our testimony to the reality of the Body and our commitment to the life of the Body. By this we declare that everything is for the Body and nothing is for the individual. If the Lord cares to use us, praise Him; if He chooses to use another, praise Him still. There is no room for jealousy in the Body of Christ.

THE ANOINTING AND PRAYER OF THE ELDERS

In James 5:14-16 we see the laying on of hands in relation to sickness. In the case of sickness we are instructed by James to call for the elders of the church. The elders, rather than the members of the church who have the gift of healing, need to be called because the sick persons in this case need to be brought under the anointing; their case must be dealt with by the representatives of the church. The sins referred to in verse 15 are particular sins; they are sins against the Body. How do we know that the sickness here is a special kind of sickness and not ordinary sickness? If we know the remedy that a doctor prescribes, then we can deduce the type of illness that a patient has. Since the patient is brought under the anointing, we can safely infer that the patient's sickness was due to a departure from the anointing. The Word of God plainly declares that many are weak and sick, and many have even died, because of the failure to discern the Lord's Body (1 Cor. 11:29-30). James 5 presents such a case. If we are living in the realm of the Body, then we are always under the anointing of the Head. However, as soon as we take an individual line, we depart from the anointing and expose ourselves to sickness and death. The sin of the man in James 5 must have been the sin of detaching himself from the Body. If his sin was only a personal sin, he could have been forgiven by trusting in the blood and by confessing to others. There would have been no need to ask the elders to anoint him with oil. The elders' oil cannot remove sin; only the blood can remove sin. Verse 15 says that he will be forgiven if he has sinned; however, the forgiveness is due to the elders' prayer. Therefore, this sin is not an ordinary sin; it is the sin of acting contrary to the Body. As a consequence, there is the need to ask the elders of the church to pray for him and to anoint him with oil in the name of the Lord so that he can be brought back under the Head and into the Body.

Verse 16 says, "Therefore confess your sins to one another and pray for one another that you may be healed." This verse tells us to confess our sins to one another. We have to confess to one another because something is wrong in the Body of Christ. The sphere of confession corresponds with the sphere of transgression. If I have only sinned against God, I must make my confession to Him alone. The sin in these verses is a sin against the Body. Since something has gone wrong in the Body of Christ, both the sick one and the elders have to take responsibility for it. The sick one has offended the Body, and the elders represent the Body. Therefore, the sick one has to confess, and the elders also have to confess. Note that confession is mutual. The sick one confesses, but the elders also confess. The sick one acknowledges that the sickness is a result of taking an individual position, and the elders acknowledge that they have failed in the matter of love and watchfulness; otherwise, the sick one would not have departed from the ground of the Body.

After the mutual confession, there is prayer. "Pray for one another." This means that the elders pray for the sick, and the sick pray for the elders. The result is that the sin is forgiven, and the sickness is healed. Mutuality is the characteristic of the Body. Do you see how the Body is highlighted in anointing, confession, and prayer? In the Body every member should have love and humility. Being outside the Body brings in not only physical sickness but also spiritual sickness. Those who are outside of the Body should see the importance of turning back to the anointing and turning back to the Body. It is through these turns that they will receive the help of the other members.

THE REVELATION PAUL RECEIVED
AT THE TIME OF HIS CONVERSION

In the case of Paul's conversion we have a further illustration of the laying on of hands. Acts 9 shows us two characteristics of the revelation that Paul received at the time of his conversion. When the Lord appeared to Paul on the way to Damascus, He showed him that persecuting the believers was the same as persecuting Him (vv. 3-5). The Lord asked, "Why are you persecuting Me?" He did not ask, "Why are you persecuting those who believe in Me?" Paul asked, "Who are You, Lord?" The Lord said, "I am Jesus, whom you persecute." The Lord showed Paul that he was persecuting the Head when he was persecuting the members of the Body. When you damage any member of the Body, you damage the Head. Every sin that offends the Body offends the Head. Every believer of the Lord is one with the Lord. This is the oneness of the Head with the Body. Paul was the first one who saw the Body of Christ. The day that the Lord revealed Himself was the day that Paul saw the Body.

After this high revelation, the Lord charged him to go into the city, and there it would be told to him what he must do (v. 6). This was also a revelation of the Body. After such a high revelation, the Lord did not speak to him directly; rather, He committed him to the Body. On the day Paul was saved, the Lord showed him the principle of the Body. Three days later the Lord sent a small disciple by the name of Ananias to lay hands on him, and Ananias said to him, "Saul, brother, the Lord has sent me—Jesus, who appeared to you on the road on which you were coming—so that you may receive your sight and be filled with the Holy Spirit" (v. 17). Ananias was just an ordinary brother. We know nothing about his history before or after this event. When he was sent by the Lord to Saul, he said, "Saul, brother." This ushered Saul into the Body of Christ, filled him with the Holy Spirit, and brought him under the anointing.

THE JUDGMENT OF TWO OR THREE BROTHERS

Matthew 18:15-16 is not about whether a person is right or wrong. It is not even about whether a person feels that he is right or wrong. It is about the testimony of two or three brothers. If they say that you are wrong, you are wrong. Therefore, when other brothers say that you are wrong, and you do not feel that you are wrong, you should take their judgment and believe in them more than in yourself. If two or three brothers stand in the name of the Lord and say something to you, you should listen to them.

In the church there are four groups of people representing the Body. They are: (1) the apostles, (2) the elders, (3) those whom the Lord has specially chosen, and (4) two or three believers who deny themselves and who have come under the

Lord's name. These four groups of people represent the church. If we are wrong, the Lord will send a believer to us to speak to us about it. If we do not listen to the word of one believer, he will tell two or three other believers. If we still do not listen to their word, we should receive help from the elders. We cannot have any independent actions. For problems that cannot be solved, we should consult the apostles. They are designated by the Lord to represent the Body. We cannot overlook the Body, and we cannot overlook the representatives of the Body. May the Lord grant us the revelation of the Body so that we can submit to Christ the Head as well as to the representatives of the Body.

CHAPTER TEN

THE RICHES IN THE BODY

Scripture Reading: Deut. 32:30; Psa. 133; Eph. 1:23; 2:20-22;
3:10, 18-19; 4:13; 6:11; 1 Cor. 12:27; Matt. 18:15-18

THE MEASURE OF CHRIST

The riches of Christ are too profound. He is the Lord who
fills all in all (Eph. 1:23). With Him are the unsearchable
riches (3:8). God's intention is not for these riches to remain
just in Christ but for these profound and infinite riches to
become the riches of the church. His intention is that the
church would become the fullness of the One who fills all in
all (1:23). The church is a vessel to contain the life of Christ.
All the riches of the Son of God are deposited in the church.
The riches of Christ are the riches of the Body of Christ.
No individual could ever contain those riches, nor could a
multitude of individuals. It takes a corporate company to hold
the riches of Christ. The individual pieces of a crashed
tumbler may hold a few drops of water, but it takes the whole
tumbler to hold a full glass of water.

The church is not a heap of stones, nor a mass of unrelated
individuals, but a "building" in which the stones are "fitted
together" so that they become "a dwelling place of God in
spirit" (2:21-22). This temple is "built upon the foundation of
the apostles and prophets" (v. 20). In a lesser sense each
individual believer is a temple of God, but only the corporate
temple can contain all the riches of God.

Ephesians 3:10 tells us that the showing forth of the
multifarious wisdom of God to the rulers and the authorities
is given to the church, not to any individual. Verses 18 and 19
say that God will cause us to be "full of strength to apprehend
with all the saints what the breadth and length and height

and depth are and to know the knowledge-surpassing love of Christ." The love of Christ is so rich that it takes the church to measure it. Christ is not only in each member, but He is also in the Body. No one member of the Body of Christ can contain all the riches of Christ. The riches of Christ that we receive individually are two-dimensional at the most, but the riches of Christ that the church receives are three-dimensional. Only the Body of Christ has the capacity to express the riches of Christ. We need to be in the Body so that we can apprehend the riches which Christ has in His Body. It is not one believer, but "all" the believers together who "arrive at the oneness of the faith and of the full knowledge of the Son of God, at a full-grown man, at the measure of the stature of the fullness of Christ" (4:13). In chapter six we are told to put on "the whole armor of God" that we may wage warfare against the hosts of darkness. However, the equipment for the fight is not given to one believer; it is given to the church. "The whole armor" can only be put on by the Body, not just by one member. Spiritual warfare is in this principle—one will chase a thousand and two will put ten thousand to flight (Deut. 32:30). The so-called church has not defeated the enemy's host, because Christians are living scattered lives instead of functioning in the Body.

Mathematically speaking, if one can chase a thousand, two should only be able to chase two thousand. But in spiritual mathematics, one chases a thousand while two chase ten thousand. The strength of two persons put together is five times that of two who are considered separately. Two is the minimum corporate number. If two persons chase the enemy separately, they will not defeat ten thousand. This is a principle: The strength of the corporate Body is very great. God cares for the corporate Body. He does not care how much strength you have or how powerful you are as an individual. As long as you are an individual and not joined to others, you can only chase a thousand. But if you are joined to others, your strength will be increased fivefold. You have to see that you are only a member. You are limited and short. You need the other members.

"For there Jehovah commanded the blessing: / Life forever"

(Psa. 133:3). Where did God command the blessing? He commanded the blessing where brothers dwell in unity (v. 1). When the Body is under the anointing, life flows freely from the Head to all the members. Christ is not the Head of any mission or organization, He is only the Head of His church. The Head is only Head over the Body. Unless we are standing on the ground of the Body, we cannot claim the headship of Christ, and if we cannot claim the full authority of the Head, we cannot know the fullness of life that streams from the Head. The blessing that is commanded whenever brothers are united under the anointing is "life forever," a full, free, unceasing stream of life.

THE LOCAL CHURCH BEING THE MANIFESTATION OF THE BODY OF CHRIST ON EARTH

When Paul wrote to a group of believers in Corinth, he said, "Now you are the body of Christ" (1 Cor. 12:27). The Body of Christ is not only universal; it is also local. Every local church is the manifestation of the Body of Christ in that locality. All of the riches of Christ are vested in the local church. The authority of the Head is vested in the local expression of the Body. Apostles and elders in the local church are representative members of the Body, but they are not the Body. The entire company of believers in a locality, not just a section of the believers, constitutes the church in that locality. The church is not one member; it represents the whole Body in a locality. Hence, when we touch the local church, we touch the Body. Participating in the fellowship of the local church is participating in the fellowship of the Body of Christ. The Body of Christ is not something abstract or unfathomable; the Body of Christ is manifested in the local churches. Anyone who wants to live in the Body in a practical way has to be in the local churches. He should fellowship with the local saints, be edified in the local church, and be built up together in mutuality.

GOD'S WILL BEING EXPRESSED IN THE LOCAL CHURCH

When Christ was on earth He referred to the church two

times—in Matthew 16 and Matthew 18. In the first instance, He referred to the universal church, and in the second instance, He referred to the local church. In speaking of the authority of the local church, He said, "If he refuses to hear the church also, let him be to you just like the Gentile and the tax collector" (18:17). This verse shows us that the authority of the church is derived from its representation of Christ. Christ has given His authority to the church and authorized the church to execute His will on earth. The Bible shows us that there are three ways in which a person can receive guidance from God: (1) God's Word—the Bible, (2) the indwelling Holy Spirit, and (3) the church in a locality. The third line is the most important line. The leading of the Bible and the Spirit are individual in nature, but the leading of the local church is corporate in nature. The local church, being the local expression of the Body of Christ, has the headship of Christ and, therefore, can know the mind of Christ, which is always communicated to His Body. The local church declares the headship of Christ. "Truly I say to you, Whatever you bind on the earth shall have been bound in heaven, and whatever you loose on the earth shall have been loosed in heaven" (v. 18). A person who sees the Body seeks fellowship and accepts the leading of the church. Often the decision of a church in a rural area is proven to be better than the decision of a church in the city. Such a decision does not originate from man's ability or wisdom but from the corporate seeking in one accord. In order to know God's will and His way, it is not enough for us to read the Bible or pray by ourselves. We have to be in the fellowship of the local church, live the Body life, and follow God's leading in the Body.

THE LOCAL CHURCH
EXECUTING THE AUTHORITY OF THE BODY

In a local church, God has established the elders as representatives of His authority. But this does not mean that they are everything. The elders should not monopolize anything; they are merely the overseers in the church. They stand on the side to guide the saints on, to stop improper activities, and to encourage proper activities so that the whole Body can be activated. Acts 12:5 says, "So then Peter was kept in the prison; but prayer was being made fervently by the church to God concerning him." Today the church should pray fervently for world events and the state of our nation. This kind of prayer involves the exercise of the authority that God has given the Body.

Much revelation has been lost to the church because believers have sought light individually instead of seeking light in the sanctuary. When a man does not see the Body, he loses many blessings. This is a great loss to the church. May the Lord show us what the Body is so that we can live in the Body and receive the riches of the Body. When we are in the Body, we know God's will, have the authority of the Body, and experience the power of the Body.

CHAPTER ELEVEN

THE MINISTRY IN THE BODY

Scripture Reading: 1 Cor. 12:4-31

SEEING THE REVELATION
OF THE BODY

A Christian must see not only that he is a believer but also that he is a member of the Body. Since he is a member, he needs other members. It is impossible for one member to live without other members. In order for a member to survive, he needs to have other members. Many people leave the denominations because they realize that denominationalism is wrong. But this is not enough; they must go on to see the Body and get into the Body. The church is not a denominational organization; the church is the living Body of Christ. A Christian is not a member of a denomination but a member of the Body of Christ. We have to see that we are members in the Body and that we cannot be separated from other members. We cannot be independent, and we cannot go on without the other members.

THE MINISTRY OF THE MEMBERS

The Body of Christ is built up by the mutual supply of the members. In addition to seeing that we are members, we have to see that every member has a ministry. Every member in the Body has a special function, and that function is its ministry. The verb form of the word *ministry* means "to serve." The ministry of a member is the special portion that a member receives from Christ. With this special portion he supplies the Body, and this is the service of the members. The Body is Christ, so our ministry is simply Christ. Everyone who belongs to the Lord has a special portion which he has received from Christ, and each portion has its characteristic feature. This feature becomes the special characteristic of his service. Ministerial service to others is based on the Christ one has within him. One does not serve others with the doctrine that he understands; he can only supply the Body with what he has received of Christ. The measure of our ministry is determined by the measure of Christ in us. Our ministry is based on these two factors: the Christ we have gained and the aspects of Christ that we have gained which are different from what other members have gained. If we only knew Christ in the same general way, what would there be for us to minister to one another? What would we have that would enable us to build up the Body? That is the most basic consideration in all ministries.

A Christian needs a ministry that is particularly his, not just a general ministry. We must gain something of Christ that others have not gained. It is this particular gain that enables us to make up that which is lacking in other members. Ministry involves a special knowledge of Christ; it is not a general knowledge of Him. Every organ in the body has its special function. The eyes see, the ears hear, and the nose smells. Every organ has its special function. In other words, every organ has its special portion. Other organs may temporarily do what another member does, but they are not dedicated to that particular function. For example, you can sometimes use your mouth to pick up things, but you cannot dedicate the mouth to this use. If the ears do not function according to their particular capacity, the body will not hear anything, and the growth of the body will be frustrated. If you have acquired something special and have some special knowledge of the Lord, you can supply the Body with it. If you have a special knowledge of the Lord, this special knowledge will constitute your specific ministry. Only specific ministries can serve the Body and cause the Body to grow. This is why every member has to continually seek and gain from the Lord what the Body does not have and convey it to the Body. When every member fulfills its ministry, there will be growth in the Body of Christ.

SEEKING TO KNOW AND EXPERIENCE THE LORD

First Corinthians 12 tells us that all the members should seek the gifts and ministries. God's intention is to have special members fulfill special ministries, using them as channels for the Lord's life to flow into the Body and to increase the measure of the Body through them. When the life we receive from the Lord flows into the Body, the measure of the stature of the Body increases. God increases the measure of the stature of the Body through the members. Madame Guyon, Mrs. Penn-Lewis, Brother T. Austin-Sparks, and others are members who have a special knowledge of Christ. Through these ones God has dispensed many riches of life into the Body. Every member should learn and know something specific before the Lord so that each one can have a specific ministry. Without a ministry, it is useless to talk about gifts. Many people stress gifts, as though gifts constitute our ministry. But our ministry is Christ; our gifts are only the means by which we minister. Two persons may use the same kind of spoon to feed a child, but whether or not the child is well-nourished will be determined by the substance in the spoon, not by the kind of spoon. We do not impart our gifts to the church; we impart Christ. Our gifts are merely the means by which we impart Him. What we minister to the Body is Christ, and what the Body receives is Christ, because Christ is all and in all in the Body.

Specific ministry comes when we receive special experiences, particular dealings, and particular discipline from the Holy Spirit. Such experiences, dealings, and discipline result in specific knowledge of Christ. With this knowledge we serve the church through the exercise of the gifts. We need to receive power from the Holy Spirit and serve the Christ we know to the church through the operation of this power. The whole matter of our ministry is a matter of life. We do not despise gifts, but it is ministry that directs the gifts, not gifts that direct the ministry. If we have a gift without first having a ministry, we will be led away by the gift and not be able to render help to the Body. What the Body lacks today is ministry, not gift. We must first discover the specific ministry that the Lord has appointed to us. Only then should we seek for the gifts to equip us to fulfill that ministry.

FIRST LIFE, THEN DOCTRINES

Our service in the Body of Christ is based on our knowledge of Christ. This knowledge comes from our experience of life, not from doctrines. God first gives us life and then doctrines. Life comes first, and doctrines follow. The Bible shows us that Abraham had a special contribution for the Body along the line of faith. This did not come by a teaching he received concerning faith, and it was not brought about by him communicating a doctrine to others. Instead, it came about by Abraham being brought into a set of circumstances in which he learned to trust God. What was wrought into him through the fires of affliction was eventually ministered by him to the whole Body for its enrichment. First there was the life and lesson of faith and then the doctrine of faith. How did Martin Luther become competent to teach the church concerning the truth that "the righteous one shall live by his faith" (Hab. 2:4)? He did not become competent by diligently studying the Bible as a textbook and then communicating the knowledge he had acquired; rather, he became competent through much suffering and affliction. When his knees were worn from kneeling and his hope for justification was gone, the Lord revealed to him in a living way that a man is justified by faith. After he had this experience, he gained the doctrine of justification by faith. Doctrine is necessary, but doctrine should follow experience, not precede it. First there should be life, and then doctrine should follow. First there should be the experience, and then there should be the teaching. The order of the New Testament is first the Gospels (facts) and then the Epistles (doctrines). First, we have the life of Christ, and then we have the teachings of Christ. We should not spend all of our time studying, analyzing, and investigating a doctrine; these are works of reeds and will fail when the test comes. The only thing that is useful is what God has wrought in us, and only this can render supply to others. The only way we can communicate to others in a living way is to communicate that which we have learned through experience. Discipline, suffering, and trials are the means for God to constitute the word into us so that we may have something to give to the Body. If we want to be ministers for the building up of the Body of Christ, we must not shrink from any trial, discipline, or dealing.

FIRST CORINTHIANS 12

First Corinthians 12:4-30 is divided into four sections:

(1) Subject—vv. 4-6: Gift, ministry, and function.

(2) The gifts of the Holy Spirit—vv. 7-11: The main emphasis being on the Holy Spirit.

(3) The ministry of the Lord—vv. 12-27: The main emphasis being on Christ.

(4) The work of God—vv. 28-30: The main emphasis being on God.

The beginning of every section points out the main divisions, while the theme can be seen in the subject of that section. Gift is related to the Holy Spirit, whereas ministry is related to Christ. The bringing forth of the ministry is through the gift of the Holy Spirit. The gifts are the vessels to perfect the ministries for the building up of the Body of Christ. The goal of the gifts is to bring in the ministries, and through the ministries, the Christ that the church has learned, known, and gained is dispensed to others. Most of the revival movements today have gifts but no ministry. It is useless to exercise gifts all day long. We have to realize that gifts are secondary; the main thing is the ministry. Once we have a ministry, we can serve the Body and cause the growth of the Body.

MUTUAL INFLUENCE OF THE MEMBERS

All the members of the Body of Christ mutually affect one another. If one member suffers, all the other members spontaneously suffer. Sometimes we feel strong because strength from other members has been transmitted to us. Every member can affect the other members. This is why we should not live by ourselves but hold the Head and seek fellowship. God conveys life to the Body through every member. If life stops in you, you will not be able to supply others with life, and the church will suffer. Every individual failure causes damage to the church. As a consequence, when one member suffers in the Body of Christ, all the members suffer with him. Every member affects other members one way or another. Hence, we have to be in the fellowship of the Body in everything we do. If we have some good experiences, it is for rendering a supply to the Body. If we are in some adverse condition, we must realize that this also affects other members of the Body.

IN THE BODY, THROUGH THE BODY, AND FOR THE BODY

Everything we have is in the Body, through the Body, and for the Body. In 1925 Brother T. Austin-Sparks was invited to America. He met a sister there who had learned many lessons through her illnesses and who had subsequently rendered much help to many people. She had a ministry of life and was a person who supplied others with life. The lessons she learned were learned in the Body, through the Body, and for the Body. This is the kind of person God is looking for today. Our living should be in the Body, through the Body, and for the Body; this should be our standard. May the Lord deliver us from individualism into the Body. May the Lord show us the Body, and may we serve His Body with a ministry which is based on our knowledge of Christ.